THE TRAGIC TRIP
OF THE DONNER PARTY

by John Micklos, Jr. • illustrated by DANNY

CAPSTONE PRESS
a capstone imprint

Published by Capstone Press, an imprint of Capstone
1710 Roe Crest Drive, North Mankato, Minnesota 56003
capstonepub.com

Library of Congress Cataloging-in-Publication Data is available on the Library of Congress website.

ISBN: 9781666390704 (hardcover)
ISBN: 9781666390650 (paperback)
ISBN: 9781666390667 (ebook PDF)

Summary: In the spring of 1846, the Donner and Reed families joined a wagon train for California in hopes of a better life. But when the party took an untested shortcut, it set them down a tragic path. Trapped by snow while crossing the Sierra Nevada mountains, they faced a winter of starvation and a desperate struggle to survive.

Editorial Credits
Editor: Abby Huff; Designer: Dina Her; Production Specialist: Tori Abraham

All internet sites appearing in back matter were available and accurate when this book was sent to press.

TABLE OF CONTENTS

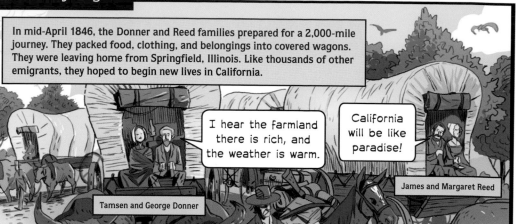

In mid-April 1846, the Donner and Reed families prepared for a 2,000-mile journey. They packed food, clothing, and belongings into covered wagons. They were leaving home from Springfield, Illinois. Like thousands of other emigrants, they hoped to begin new lives in California.

I hear the farmland there is rich, and the weather is warm.

California will be like paradise!

Tamsen and George Donner

James and Margaret Reed

On May 12, the families set out on the Oregon Trail. The trail began in Independence, Missouri. It crossed prairies, rivers, and mountains to Oregon. Some emigrants, like the Donners and Reeds, would branch off southwest to California.

The trip takes six months.

We should still reach California before winter.

Others started west earlier than us.

The Donner and Reed families soon joined a larger wagon train. Day after day, wagons lurched along. Great herds of buffalo provided food.

KKRACK

By July 12, the wagon train reached Independence Rock in what's now Wyoming. They had traveled 820 miles in two months.

We are all doing well and are in high spirits.

The journey was almost halfway done. But the roughest parts still lay ahead.

We must reach Sutter's Fort in California before November...

...before snow falls in the mountains.

Look. Explorer Lansford Hastings describes a shortcut that will save us hundreds of miles.

Around mid-July, the group reached the South Pass of the Rocky Mountains. Soon they would reach the point where the shortcut, Hastings Cutoff, began. The families had to make a choice.

We should take the proven route.

No, the shortcut is better. It will make sure we get across the mountains before winter.

On July 20, the Donners, Reeds, and other families left the main wagon train. In total, 20 wagons and 74 people turned onto Hastings Cutoff.

This group would become known as the Donner Party.

Days later, the Donner Party rested at Fort Bridger. The owner assured them they had made a good decision.

The cutoff has plenty of grass and water.

Lansford Hastings left here with a wagon train last week. You might be able to catch up.

On July 31, the Donner Party left Fort Bridger. Travel went smoothly. After a week, the emigrants reached a canyon. They found a note left by Hastings.

I will ride ahead to Hastings for more details.

He says it's hard to get wagons through. He says there's an easier way.

The canyon was filled with boulders, trees, and brush. James Reed caught up with Hastings and the wagon train.

In that direction lies an easier route through the mountains. Your group should take it.

The "easier" route still proved difficult. The Donner Party had to hack down bushes and trees to create a path. It took two and a half weeks to travel about 30 miles.

They worried about the time they had lost.

On the way, the party also lost a life. Luke Halloran died from illness. But the Graves family had joined the group. They brought 3 new wagons and 13 new people.

Let's hope the rest of us reach California safely.

Poor Luke.

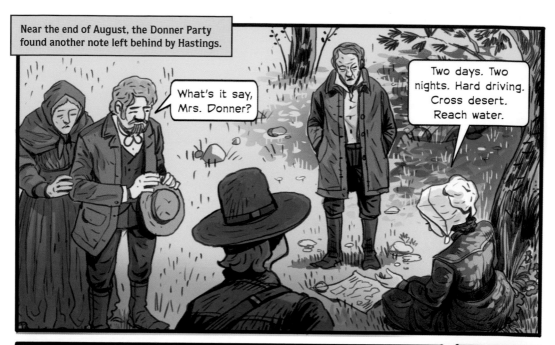

Near the end of August, the Donner Party found another note left behind by Hastings.

What's it say, Mrs. Donner?

Two days. Two nights. Hard driving. Cross desert. Reach water.

On August 30, the Donner Party started across the Great Salt Lake Desert in Utah. They walked through blistering days and suffered freezing nights.

We've walked mile after mile. Every step seems to be the very last we will take!

James Reed rode ahead to search for water. He returned with some a few days later. But he received bad news.

The cattle and oxen have stampeded. They are lost.

I warned you to watch them! Now we have no way to move our wagons!

After five long days (not the two days Hastings had promised), the emigrants came out of the desert. They rested. They took stock of their supplies.

We left behind two wagons. But at least we survived.

Other families lost cattle, oxen, and wagons too.

The group realized they might run short of food before reaching California.

We are counting on you, Stanton and McCutchen.

We'll ride ahead to Sutter's Fort. We'll bring back supplies.

At the end of September, the Donner Party reached the Humboldt River in what's now Nevada. Here, their path met up with the trail other emigrants had taken. The group began to argue.

The shortcut wasn't short at all.

We've traveled more than 100 extra miles!

We are far behind schedule, Reed!

It's not my fault Hastings gave bad advice.

Tensions grew among the tired emigrants. They now traveled in family groups.

On October 5, the ox teams of James Reed and John Snyder got tangled.

You are moving too slowly, Snyder. I want to get by.

Why--!

After Snyder hit Reed's wife, Reed's knife flashed.

He struck Snyder in the chest.

Minutes later, Snyder lay dead.

The Donner Party continued west. Soon the group had more losses. On October 9, old Mr. Hardcoop went missing. He had no wagon and could not keep up on foot.

We should look for him.

We don't have time. We must keep moving.

Most Indigenous people the group met on the trail were friendly. But the Paiute tribe objected to settlers crossing their lands. They stole or killed many of the Donner Party's animals. William and Eleanor Eddy had to abandon their wagon.

Our oxen are dead. Now we have no choice but to walk.

We can do it, William.

Mr. Wolfinger had to leave his wagon as well. He stayed behind to cache his belongings. Two men helped him. They later returned to camp. Mr. Wolfinger did not.

Paiutes killed him, Mrs. Wolfinger.

I believe you killed my husband in order to take his money.

In late October, the emigrants rejoiced.

Look, it's Charles Stanton!

Stanton had come back from Sutter's Fort. With him were two Miwok guides sent by John Sutter. They brought mules and much-needed food.

Thank goodness! I feared we would soon run out of food. Where is McCutchen?

He became ill and stayed behind. But I passed James Reed. He promised to bring more supplies.

Fed and rested, the emigrants began their journey across the Sierra Nevada mountain range. Then an axle broke on a Donner wagon. George badly cut his hand making repairs.

I should clean this cut before I wrap it.

There's no time. Stanton said he saw snow in the mountains. We must cross before more falls.

By the end of October, most of the Donner Party had reached a mountain lake. They had traveled nearly 2,000 miles. They had a little more than 100 miles to go.

Once they made it across the Sierra Nevada summit, the trip to Sutter's Fort would be downhill.

But the emigrants found snow ahead. Some set off for the mountain pass. As they went, the snow grew deeper.

The wagons are stuck. Leave them!

They packed their belongings onto oxen. They pushed forward.

Stanton walked on in the chest-deep snow. He managed to reach the summit in the evening.

It's only a mile or so to the top. Let's cross tonight!

We're too tired. Let's wait till morning.

More snow fell overnight. Some drifts reached higher than the emigrants' heads.

It's no use! We must go back!

They struggled down to the lake.

It's not really winter yet. We'll wait for warmer days. The snow will melt.

The group did not realize they had missed their best chance at safely crossing the mountain. Their decision proved fateful for all. For some, it would be fatal.

Patrick Breen's family moved into a cabin left by a previous traveler. Other families built shelters. In all, 59 people camped near the lake.

I hope we won't be here long!

The Donners never caught up with the rest of the group. Trapped by the snow, they built rough shelters near a creek. They were about 6 miles away from the lake. There were 22 people in this camp.

After days of snow, the sun came out. Some emigrants tried to go up the mountain. They failed to reach the top.

If only we had crossed when we had the chance.

On November 22, a group set out again. They nearly reached the summit. Then the mules got stuck.

We must save people, not animals. Leave the mules, Stanton!

No! I promised to return them to John Sutter.

They turned back.

More snow fell on November 26, Thanksgiving Day. The emigrants had little to celebrate.

I am thankful we are still alive.

By December 1, some emigrants were running low on food. Many of the remaining cattle had died and were lost under deep snow.

I hope that help comes from Sutter's Fort soon.

I hope so as well.

Help was not coming. The men at Sutter's Fort thought winter travel was too dangerous. They believed the emigrants had enough supplies to last till spring.

These snowshoes should make walking easier.

We can get help.

Without enough food, many emigrants grew weak and ill. A few died.

Some of the healthiest people prepared to try to cross the mountain once again.

On December 16, a group of 17 people left camp. It included emigrant men, women, and children, as well as the two Miwok guides.

With luck, we may reach help in about a week.

The group struggled through the deep snow even with snowshoes. Two people without the shoes soon turned back.

I can only see snow and trees, Stanton.

I remember the route from my earlier trip. I will guide us.

After two days, the group reached the mountaintop.

The snowshoers had only enough food for six days. Each person got three small strips of dried beef daily. But Stanton grew weak. He lagged behind. By the sixth day, he did not catch up to camp.

What now, Eddy? We've lost our guide.

And the Miwoks say they can't recognize the way with so much snow.

We keep heading west.

By late December, the snowshoers had been walking for nearly two weeks. They had been caught in a sudden storm. Four had died from starvation.

The survivors faced a terrible decision.

We need food. We must eat the dead.

I--I don't know if I can.

It's the only way.

The snowshoers ate the dead. They gained some strength to keep moving west.

A few days later, another person died. The group ate that body too. They dried meat for the journey ahead.

But the group soon faced starvation again. William Foster took a drastic step. He murdered the Miwok men, Luis and Salvador. The others did nothing to stop him. They ate the bodies.

In mid-January, the snowshoers came to a small Indigenous village. The villagers had little food. Still, they shared some with the strangers.

Days later, William Eddy finally reached help at Johnson's Ranch.

Help! Others are still out there.

Only seven snowshoers survived. It took them more than a month to travel 70 miles.

Because of their hardships, the group became known as the Forlorn Hope.

Meanwhile, emigrants at the lake also suffered. They were slowly starving. Still, on December 25, Margaret Reed gave her children a Christmas feast. She had set aside some dried apples, beans, and bacon.

But most days, the emigrants ate soup made of boiled ox hide. Some families still had a little meat from their cattle and oxen. Others ate their pets and the covers off of books.

By the end of January, people were dying of starvation and illness. They prayed for rescuers to come.

Heavy snow continued throughout the winter.

I hope we will live to see the bare surface of the earth once more.

By mid-February, the surviving emigrants knew there were only two possible outcomes—rescue or death.

I feel like we will soon go to sleep and never wake up again!

The people at Sutter's Fort soon learned about the Forlorn Hope group of snowshoers. They now knew the Donner Party needed help. By early February, two rescue teams had left the fort. James Reed traveled with the second team.

I pray my family is still alive!

The rescuers struggled through the snow, just as the emigrants had.

We must hurry if we are to save them!

On February 18, the first rescue team reached the lake camp. They saw only snowdrifts.

Hello?

Then people came out of their shelters.

Some emigrants laughed. Others wept. After more than three and a half months, help had finally arrived.

Are you angels from heaven?

No, but we are here to help.

The rescuers had to make hard choices. Some people at the camp were too weak to travel.

I hate to leave anyone.

We can't take people who can't keep up.

On February 22, more than 20 emigrants began the journey to Johnson's Ranch. The trip over the mountains was still dangerous. John Denton died on the way. So did 3-year-old Ada Keseberg.

The two rescue teams soon crossed paths. James Reed saw his wife and two of his children among the survivors.

They have a death-like look. But thank God they are alive!

Father!

James!

Reed and the second rescue team arrived at the lake camp on March 1. They found human bones there. As the Forlorn Hope group had done, some emigrants had turned to cannibalism to survive.

How could they do this?!

We cannot judge them. I can't imagine having to make such a decision.

There was joy as well as sorrow at the camps. Reed found his other two children, starving but alive. His entire family had made it through the winter.

I was afraid I would never see you again.

In mid-March, a third rescue team arrived. Tamsen Donner refused to leave her dying husband, George.

If you stay, you both will die.

That is my choice.

Rescuers led more survivors to safety. Five people remained in the camps.

I did what I had to.

A final rescue team reached the camp in mid-April. Lewis Keseberg was the only living person left. He had survived by eating the dead.

The previous summer, 87 emigrants had taken Hastings Cutoff. By April 1847, a little more than half survived to settle in California. They had finally reached paradise, but the memories of their terrible journey would never leave them.

We lost everything, but I don't care. We have got through with our lives.

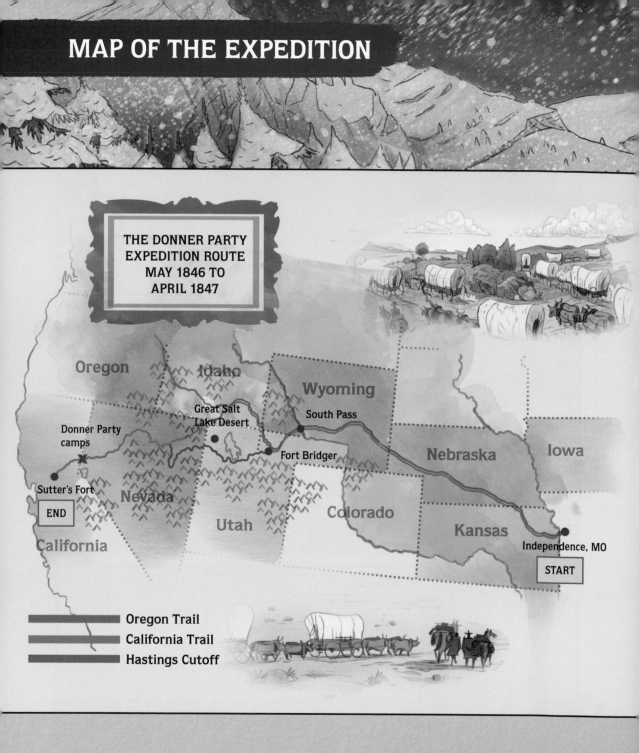

THE DONNER PARTY
EXPEDITION ROUTE
MAY 1846 TO
APRIL 1847

Oregon

Idaho

Wyoming

Great Salt
Lake Desert

South Pass

Donner Party
camps

Fort Bridger

Nebraska

Iowa

Sutter's Fort

Nevada

END

California

Utah

Colorado

Kansas

Independence, MO

START

Oregon Trail
California Trail
Hastings Cutoff

MORE ABOUT THE EXPEDITION

Bad advice. Bad decisions. Bad luck. The Donner Party experienced them all. The emigrants had dreamed of a better life in California. Instead, they faced starvation in the mountains. Nearly half of the group died.

Most of those who settled in California did well. All members of the Reed and Breen families survived. The Reeds moved to San Jose. James became wealthy during the California Gold Rush. He donated the land where San Jose State University sits today. His daughter Virginia later wrote about the trip west.

The Breens settled in San Juan Batista, California. Patrick Breen ran an inn and a ranch. He served as the town's postmaster. When Patrick died, he left an estate worth more than $100,000. That equals nearly $2 million today.

George and Tamsen Donner's children were taken in by other families. Eliza Donner later wrote a book about her journey to California.

As many as 400,000 people traveled on the Oregon Trail between the mid-1840s and mid-1860s. The Donner Party is one of the most well-known groups to head west. Places in the Sierra Nevada are named after them. Those places include Donner Summit, Donner Pass, and Donner Lake. But the Donner Party's trip was also the most tragic.

GLOSSARY

axle (AK-suhl)—a rod that passes through the center of a wheel and allows it to turn

banish (BAN-ish)—to send away as a punishment

cache (KASH)—to hide or store something with the hope of returning for it later

cannibalism (KAN-ih-buh-liz-uhm)—the act of a person eating human flesh

canyon (KAN-yun)—a deep, narrow area with steep sides

emigrant (EM-ih-gruhnt)—a person who travels from their home area to live somewhere else

forlorn (for-LORN)—sad

Indigenous (in-DIJ-uh-nuhss)—a way to describe the first people who lived in a certain area

paradise (PAR-uh-dahys)—a beautiful, perfect place

stampede (stam-PEED)—to run wildly out of control

starvation (star-VAY-shuhn)—dying or being in great pain from lack of food

summit (SUM-it)—the highest point on a mountain

READ MORE

Enz, Tammy. *Science on the Oregon Trail*. North Mankato, MN: Capstone, 2021.

Oachs, Emily Rose. *Death in the Donner Party: A Cause-and-Effect Investigation*. Minneapolis: Lerner Publications, 2016.

Philbrick, Rodman. *Stay Alive: The Journal of Douglas Allen Deeds, The Donner Party Expedition, 1846*. New York: Scholastic, 2021.

INTERNET SITES

EyeWitness to History: The Tragic Fate of the Donner Party, 1847
eyewitnesstohistory.com/donnerparty.htm

History: 10 Things You Should Know About the Donner Party
history.com/news/10-things-you-should-know-about-the-donner-party

The Oregon Trail
oregontrail101.com/index.html

AUTHOR BIO

John Micklos, Jr. has written more than 60 children's books spanning a wide range of ages and genres. His work includes picture books, poetry books, and numerous nonfiction books. He enjoys visiting schools and conducting writing workshops with students.

ILLUSTRATOR BIO

DANNY is a freelance artist born and raised in Rome, Italy. He graduated from the IED (Europe Institute of Design), where he's now a professor. His career began as a visual and storyboard artist for advertising companies and movie productions. DANNY has since gone on to work for Usborne Publishing and many other publishing houses, illustrating historical series and fiction tales for young readers.